The Camp Counselor's Handbook of Over 90 Games and Activities Just for Rainy Days!

by David Burrow

Benjamin Publishing Company
Fredonian Street
Shirley, MA 01464

508-425-4055
800-225-0682
(outside MA)

First Edition March 1990

Library of Congress Catalog Card Number 90-081002
ISBN 0-9622191-2-6

Printed in the United States of America
by
Old Paths Tract Society, Inc.
Shoals, Indiana

Table of Contents

1

How to Create a Successful Program When It Rains

Camping with youth is an outdoor activity.

Campers come to play ball, swim, hike, explore, learn water-related skills, play games and just have a great time **OUTDOORS.**

When it rains, the camper's first emotional impression is, "The fun's all over. This day is ruined." If you wake up to the sound of pouring rain, you need to take command of the situation quickly and keep your campers' spirits high.

The purpose of this little manual is to give you lots of ideas of fun things to do on rainy days.

Look at rain as a great opportunity to do different types of activities.

Rain Is Beautiful!

"Wow! It's raining! Finally! Now we can do those special activities that have been planned ONLY if it rains!"

That's exactly what you should say to your group of campers. Get them excited about the new possibilities.

How to Create a Successful Program When It Rains

➤   **Plan ahead**. After it starts to rain, you may have your hands full of either antsy campers or depressed ones. It's too late to put together ideas and plans.

Before camp starts (perhaps as part of counselor training or before coming to camp), put together plans for rainy-day activities. Become familiar with the ideas in this manual and mark the ones that will work well in your situation.

Some activities require equipment such as paper, pencil, props, or other things. Have a complete understanding of how to conduct the activity and have the props ready.

➤   **Find out what camp facilities are available to you.** Can you use the dining hall? A special fireplace? The chapel? A separate room? The craft room? The nature den or other special places? How do you sign up for these special places or take turns with other cabin units?

➤   **FLEXIBILITY is the key to success.** You may be planning to use the fireplace in the dining hall, but another cabin needs to dry out 18 wet sneakers there. Have at least two or three alternative plans.

Take advantage of the immediate situation. For example, maybe it's a hot day with no lightning, so an outdoor activity where everybody gets soaking wet would be lots of fun.

➤   **Consider the needs of the campers.** If there have been problems with sickness, keep them dry and warm. If it is early in the week or camping session, do something active. If it is late in the week and the kids are getting worn down, take advantage of the opportunity to slow things down. If you have girls, try a discussion-group activity. What do YOUR campers need?

➤   **Keep campers fully involved.** When campers are DOING something, the total experience is much more meaningful and fulfilling. There is a place for the "Show" by the counselors and staff or the lecture by the expert, but make it the exception.

➤   **Save one to three special activities ONLY for the rain.** If it only rains once all summer, only the campers that are there for that week will get to enjoy it. But next summer, they will still remember it and help lift the spirits of others on wet days.

➤   **Work with the Program Director or Camp Director.** He/she may have several things planned for the entire camp. It may also be that the Director will look to you, and/or a committee of counselors, to plan and run an all-camp activity. Be ready.

2   All-Camp Activities

The following is a list of activities* that involves the whole camp. These activities may be initiated by the Program Director or by the counselor working with the Director. Some are very simple but add memorable moments to the total camp experience.

➤   **Sleep in.** Simply change the daily schedule so the campers can sleep in an extra 20 to 60 minutes. This will require: (a) clear notification to all counselors the night before, (b) coordination with the kitchen, (c) and adjustment of the remainder of the morning schedule. **[A]**

➤   **Breakfast in Bed.** Keep it simple, but make it special. The counselor brings the tray to the cabin/tent with juice, milk, and cold cereal (the kind you can eat right in the box). Your cooks may have other creative ideas of a simple meal. Use paper service so a trash bag takes care of the cleanup.

This will require: (a) careful coordination and prearrangement with the kitchen the night before,

---

*   The letters in brackets at the end of each activity relate to the following: **A** = all ages; **Jr.** = grade-school age; **Sr.** = junior- and senior-high age; **G** = recommended for girls only; **B** = recommended for boys only.

(b) an alteration of schedule, (c) and the arrangement for proper supervision of the campers while the counselor is getting the food from the dining hall. [A]

➤   **Special-picture Program**. Some camps keep on hand a move projector and a special film. The camp may also have pictures (slides) from last summer's camp. If you have the personnel and ability, you might even be able to put together a slide program for THIS SESSION of camp. Take pictures during the days of camp, and get them developed at a 24-hour turnaround, photo store. [A]

➤   **Indoor Track Meet**. Each cabin group is a team. They compete in mock Olympic events like the discus throw with paper plates, the javelin throw with straws, the hundred-yard dash for a short distance and back, the shot put with balloons, the long jump, high jump, standing jump, and other races and relays. [Jr.]

➤   **Progressive Game Party**. Each cabin has a game to play. The games can be of their own creation, or they may play games like toss the pennies into the hat, paper and pencil games, telling stories, or board games. Every half hour the campers rotate to the next cabin or room. One cabin could have refreshments, but this needs to be worked out with the kitchen. [Jr.]

➤ **The County Fair**. This activity takes extensive preparation and pre-planning. It can be a lot of fun if you plan adequately and get the campers involved in the total project. This is a good all-day project after days of rain.

At the county fair the campers will be free to go from booth to booth to participate in each activity. Each camper is given 12 red tokens. It costs one token for each activity. The number of tokens will depend on: (a) how many activities are created, (b) how large the camp is, and (c) how much time you are giving for this activity. So use your own judgement.

Each camper will also receive 12 blue tokens. These can be used at the concession stand. The concession stand is really lunch. How much you "charge" for food needs to be worked out so every child can have a full meal.

The red and blue tokens are all part of the fun. There is no real charge for them. They are only a way to control how often a child participates in the activities.

You will need a large open room. Usually, rearranging the dining room works best unless you have a large recreation room available. Do not forget to coordinate this with the kitchen because you will need their help.

Be prepared with plenty of props. Some of these are made by campers and staff while others are makeshift. The preparation time is all part of the fun. The more the campers do, the more they enjoy the activity.

Each cabin group is to make one booth. This can be a table, only or be more elaborate with blankets and other makeshift walls. Each booth involves an activity or tests a skill. During the fair, the campers take turns running their booth. When not running their own booth, they can participate in the fair.

At all times, at least one counselor or adult is at each booth, but the campers run it. [Jr.]

Here are some activities for the County Fair:

☞ **Feed the Clown**

Toss a been bag through a clown's mouth. The clown is drawn on a large piece of cardboard (or sheet of old paneling) and a large hole is cut for the mouth. You need been bags and a clown.

☞ **Air Show**

If there is a safe place for the campers to climb up to a high place, let them make paper airplanes and fly them from this high vantage point.

☞ **Penny Drop**

Drop the pennies into an open jar while standing on a chair or platform.

☞ **Big-ball Bowling**

Set up a few 2" x 4" x 12" blocks of wood on their end. A bowling alley is set up along one wall. One or two attempts are given to knock over all the "pins." Use a large, rubber, playground ball.

☞ **Target Shooting**

Candles are set up on one end of the table. Tape heavy tinfoil on the table under the candle-setup area. The shooting takes place with squirt guns from the other end of the table. The objective is to put out the fire on all three candles.

Keep the guns half full of water or limit the number of shots. Youngest campers get more shots.

☞ **Soft-ball Throw**

With a backdrop of a hanging blanket, set up a board with something to knock off (dolls, pop cans, wooden pins). From the throwing line, each person is given three balls.

☞ **Gold Mine**

There is no booth needed for this one. The youngest campers can hunt for the 50 (or more) pennies that have been painted gold. These are hidden all over the room.

☞ **Bust the Balloon**

A target with balloons is set up with a LARGE backdrop. Darts are used to break the balloons. Awards for more tokens are inside certain balloons. <u>Be sure the backdrop can handle the stray darts</u>. This activity must be closely supervised for safety.

☞ **Wash the Counselor**

A counselor (or other staff person) wears a poncho and sticks his head through a large hole in cardboard or paneling. The camper stands behind a firing line and tries to hit the counselor in the face with a large, soft, wet sponge.

Keep the distance great enough so it will not hurt. Move the firing line back for older or bigger campers.

☞ **Shave the Balloon**

At this booth the camper tries to shave shaving cream off a balloon. There is NO blade in the razor. If the balloon breaks, he loses.

☞ **Brainstorm**

Meet as a staff and brainstorm other activities that might be added. Here are a few starters: walk the plank, basketball with a bucket of water, frisbee target, paper folding, balancing, and "can you do this."

☞ **Concession Stand**

This, too, is a series of separate booths run by campers. It could cost one or two blue tokens for each booth. You could have pop corn, cup of drink, piece of pizza, half a sandwich, cup of soup, special dessert, or other creative ideas from your cook.

☞ **Special Acts**

Maybe a cabin group will have a skilled counselor in some special area. This cabin could have their own "show." It could be singing, skits, stunts, juggling, mock-animal exhibit, or some other creative idea.

➤   **A Night Out (a Banquet Night).** If it looks like days of rain, plan a very special meal or banquet. The possibilities seem endless. The idea is that the whole camp is getting ready for this big event. Since we are dealing with older campers, be very sensitive to avoid having a dating affair because of the few that will be left out. Handle with care! Here are some options to use with this basic idea. [Sr.]

☞ **Formal, dress-up banquet.** Decorate the dining hall. Fix up center pieces. Plan a program with heavy camper involvement.

☞ **Sadi Hawkins day.** Same as above, except the girls must ask a guy. HOW they ask can become creative - secret notes, through a friend, direct approach, coded message, trap, etc.

☞ **Special meal.** Hawaiian, hobo, nursery school, candlelight, Halloween, Christmas, or other.

➤   **Colorful Day.** At breakfast, announce that this is ORANGE DAY! Everyone should try to wear the color orange. (Choose any color that is bright). They have the option of coloring or painting something and wearing it, such as a picture or design with that color. [A]

➤ **Camper Take-over Day**. In this activity, the campers "take over" the camp by assuming the roles of the camp leadership positions — Camp Director, Program Director, Life Guard, Nurse, Counselor, and so forth.

I found that this works best in a small camp with under 70 campers. Think through carefully what you will have each camper do that is elected to these positions. Have the new "job descriptions" written down. After the election, go over with each elected camper what he or she is to do.

During the day, the camper goes with the camp leader and actually begins to learn something of what it takes to run a camp. At every opportunity, the camper is in front of the group and does the leading. View this as a learning experience for the camper. [A]

➤ **Sing!** Rain will probably cut down the amount of time needed for some of the regular camp activities. So take the extra time after meals or during the meetings to SING! Plan a real song fest by having a list ready of songs that most campers know, and be ready to teach a NEW song that few know. [A]

➤   **Special Clinics or "Seminars."** Since the rain is keeping you indoors, take the opportunity to teach something of special interest to campers. This is good for later in the camping session when a lot of activity is not needed. [A]

☞   Conduct a sports clinic in a sport that one of the staff knows well: football, soccer, tennis, basketball, archery, golf or some other sport.

☞   Offer a wrestling class for boys if you have staff members who know how to do it safely and are qualified to teach and referee.

☞   Could the cook make a cake for each cabin and have a cake decorating contest? You need small cabin groups for this one.

☞   Have a specialist in some area come and speak to the campers. Many times they have visuals to make the presentation even more interesting. Contact the forest ranger, a geologist, a nature expert, or an astronomer.

➤   **Dress the Counselor.** An hour before supper, each cabin group dresses up their counselor. It is amazing what they do! The props may include special items from the craft shop, blankets, sheets, strange hats, or even raincoats.

I still remember the big, yellow, rubber ducky (a large, Camp Pastor in a bright, yellow rain coat)! [Jr.]

➤   **One-utensil Meal.** This adds a little spice to the program, but does not take any extra time. As the campers come into the dining hall, they reach into a box and take one utensil. They cannot see what they are taking. They eat the whole meal with it. The counselors are each given one kitchen utensil — huge spoon, fork, beater, spatula and so forth. Be sure the meal being served is appropriate for this. [Jr.]

➤   **Silent Meal.** Whether raining or not, this is good for a noisy group of juniors. When they enter the dining hall, that is the end of any talking. All "conversation" must be with hand signals. The silence is deafening! [Jr.]

➤   **Backwards Day.** The campers are told when they get up (and its raining) that this will be backwards day! For breakfast (only) they dress backwards by putting clothes on backwards.

Breakfast itself becomes supper, and dessert is served first. The daily schedule may be turned around also. [Jr.]

➤   **Talent Night**. Starting at lunch, each cabin should plan on presenting some talent for a special evening program. The schedule may need to be adjusted accordingly. Keep it a talent night rather than a skit night.

There are always a variety of singing groups and solos, but what about other talents like art, story-telling, impressionists, instrumentals, or some special demonstration? [Sr.]

➤   **Table-game Time**. This can be part of the Progressive Games Party, or a special time in the dining hall or recreation room. The camp will need to have a large number of games available like Clue, Sorry, Monopoly, Checkers, Chess, Pit, UNO, and so forth. [A]

➤   **The "Big Challenge."** Hold a challenge contest. Who can do the best imitation of a cow or other animal? Who can wear the most hats? Who can stack the blocks the highest? Who can eat the pie the fastest? Who can do the most push-ups? Who can roll the egg the farthest? Who can do the most sit-ups? A staff brainstorming time will turn up many more possibilities. [A]

➤   **Kangaroo Court**. Hold this mock, court trial after a meal. The offense can be a trivial event or a created one, such as: sleeping during chapel, sneezing at breakfast, not singing, peaking during grace, growing white hair during camp, and so forth.

Be sure the one chosen to be put on trial can take it in good humor. The sentence can be just as silly as the offense, like: eating with a blind fold on, walking the plank into the pool, singing a solo, or performing some stunt. [A]

➤ **Bible Charades**. Give each cabin 15 to 30 minutes to create a Bible-story charade. As each Bible story is acted out without words, the rest of the camp tries to guess what the story is. [Jr.]

➤ **Counselor Charades**. The campers act out how certain counselors act and what they look like. The others try to guess what counselor or staff person is being represented. [A]

➤ **Skit Day**. If the rain will not quit, plan for a skit day in the middle of the afternoon. Each cabin should create a skit while in their cabin or tent. Then all of the camp should meet together to see each other's skit. [A]

➤ **Getting to Know You** (a paper and pencil game with pre-printed sheets). If the first day of camp is doused, start out with, "Find someone who...." Each camper is to find another camper who matches the description. Here are a few possibilities. Add some more of your own. [A]

- Has red hair.
- Has come the longest distance to camp.
- Loves watermelon.
- Is at camp for the first time.
- Has been to this camp more than 3 times.
- Has the biggest smile.
- Has the shortest name.
- Is the lightest in weight.
- Wonders what he will be when he grows up.
- Reads the PEANUTS comic strips.
- Has had a good laugh this week. Why?
- Has the same size clothing as you have.
- You do not know. Get to know them!
- Who would give you a backrub.

I think you get the idea. <u>Be careful to choose items that do not embarrass campers.</u> Create items that will show campers things they have in common.

3 All-Camp Activities Outside in a Warm Rain

The following is a list of activities* that involves the whole camp. These activities may be initiated by the Program Director or by the counselor working with the Director. Some are very simple but add memorable moments to the total camp experience.

Playing outside in the rain can be lots of fun.

Plan activities that MOVE and generate body heat so the campers don't get a chill. Do campers have an extra pair of sneakers or shoes? Or is the activity such that no shoes are needed? Before moving into these activities, be sure there are dry clothes and shoes available (and hopefully a warm shower).

➤ **Mud Football.** The guys love a messy game of tag football. Be sure it is properly supervised with a referee. Do not let it get too rough or out of hand. Plan for a swim in the lake (clothes and all) or a shower after the game. The girls may want to watch this one! [**Sr. B**]

---

* The letters in brackets at the end of each activity relate to the following: A = all ages; **Jr.** = grade-school age; **Sr.** = junior- and senior-high age; **G** = recommended for girls only; **B** = recommended for boys only.

➤   **Scavenger Hunt.** Plan ahead for a wet scavenger hunt. Each cabin unit is given an identical list of things to find. The goofier the list, the more they like it.

Include things that will be found because it is raining: a toad, worm, salamander. Can you put things in the pool or lake that have to be retrieved such as coins or balls (the lifeguard will need to be there)?

Other items on your list may be a piece of firewood, a tooth (from a comb!), a picture of Lincoln (from a penny!), a tree leaf common in your camp, a candy wrapper (or name other trash that has accumulated), a handful of sand, special kinds of grasses, and so forth. The first cabin to bring all the items to a designated location is the winner. [Jr.]

➤   **Cookout.** If a cookout is already planned, go for it! However, take some dry kindling and other types of fire starters. You can find dry wood by pealing off bark and by splitting wood in half. [A]

➤   **Outdoor Games.** Keep with the regular camp schedule, if this is reasonable. If recreation time is scheduled for soccer, tag, basketball or another fast moving activity, go ahead and do it in the rain. Baseball can be a drag because it doesn't move enough. [A]

➤ **Relay Races**. These can be fun if you are on grass that will give a softer landing! [A]

➤ **Swimming**. If there is no lightning in sight, plan a regular swim time, swim races, or a water carnival. [A]

4

What to Do
in the Cabin in the Rain

The following is a list of activities* that involves the whole camp. These activities may be initiated by the Program Director or by the counselor working with the Director. Some are very simple but add memorable moments to the total camp experience.

Sometimes there is a lull in the program. Or you may be waiting for the downpour to stop. It may be that the Director will tell you to plan a whole afternoon in the cabin and make it a special time with the campers. Here are some ideas to turn that time into showers of blessings.

Will these ideas work in YOUR cabin or tent or dorm full of campers? Before starting any of these activities, follow this procedure to insure a more successful time.

* The letters in brackets at the end of each activity relate to the following: **A** = all ages; **Jr.** = grade-school age; **Sr.** = junior- and senior-high age; **G** = recommended for girls only; **B** = recommended for boys only.

Five Rules for Success in Leading Games

First, plan in advance. Be ready for any activity. If it is paper and pencil, have the materials ready BEFORE introducing the game.

Second, read your group of campers. Some groups will really enjoy one activity while another group will show no interest in it. The more you understand your campers, the better you will be able to choose the activities that they will enjoy.

Third, if you are going to play a game, never tell them what you are going to do. Just take them one step at a time. For example, if your game requires their sitting in a circle, start like this:

Camper: "What are we doing?"

Counselor: "Since it's so wet outside, we're going to have a special activity right here. Now, count off starting with Mary. Now that we have an order for sitting, see if you can copy this motion and rhythm." You are into the game called "Ready Rhythm."

Fourth, if the game involves someone being "It," beware lest younger players try to fail so that they can become "It." If this becomes a problem, change the rules of the game.

Fifth, understand before starting just how YOU are going to lead this game and what the rules will be. Many games have variations and different ways to play, but only ONE way can be used. You choose that way and stick with it, even though several campers might have other ways to play the game.

➤   **Treasure Chest (Game Box)** Before camp starts, create a game box. This is a special surprise box that is opened in front of the campers ONLY WHEN AND IF it rains. They will be praying for rain!

Inside that box are ideas, table games, paper and pencil games, special stunts, and ideas for a good time. Many of the things that follow could be put into the box. For added anticipation, tell them about the box the first night of camp, but have a padlock on it. This box can only be opened in case of an emergency called rain! [Jr.]

➤   **Craft Time**. Be sure to have ready one or several craft projects that everyone can do. Work with your Craft Director to plan what to do on rainy days. KNOW what projects your cabin group will do, where to get the materials, what it will cost, and how to direct the activity toward success.

In your game box you might be able to have several crafts ready, such as paper folding, lanyards, mobiles, drawing a Bible verse, leather craft kits, a simple sewing project, jelly bean animals, bead projects, drawing and sketching. [A]

➤   **First-day Activities**. If it is raining on registration day, use it as an opportunity to draw your cabin group together. Combine these ideas with the suggestions in Chapter 2 of *How to Be a Successful Camp Counselor.*

☞   **Create a cabin slogan**. "All for one and one for all," "the best in the west," etc.

☞   **Create a cabin name**. It is best if the name and slogan are related to the theme for the camp session. Use Chapter 15 in *How to Be a Successful Camp Counselor* to draw the campers out and have them participate in this discussion.

☞   **Find a cabin Bible verse**. This will be YOUR verse for the week. You may want to take it out of the Bible series that they will have that week. Have each one write it down and post it above his or her bed, or make a fancy sign and put up in the cabin. Spend some time starting to memorize it.

☞   **Create a cabin sign to hang either outside or inside the cabin**. Have the cabin name, slogan, verse or cheerful greeting on it.

☞   Together, **create a HUGE greeting/ welcome card** for the new Camp Pastor, Camp Director, Camp Missionary or Camp Nurse.

☞   See the game "Ready Rhythm" under NONACTIVE games.

☞   See the game Zip-zap under NONACTIVE games.

5   Paper and Pencil
Games in the Cabin

The following is a list of activities* that involves the whole camp. These activities may be initiated by the Program Director or by the counselor working with the Director. Some are very simple but add memorable moments to the total camp experience.

➤   **Name Acrostics.** Put your name down the left side of the paper. For each letter of your name find...

- another name that starts with that letter.
- a Bible name that starts with that letter.
- something you can find in camp that starts with that letter. **[A]**

➤   **Word Creation.** On a large card or in large print on paper, post a word or words so all can see.

At the "GO" signal, each camper tries to create as many words as possible from the letters in the original word(s). Use a Bible name like Bethlehem, or even the name of your camp. **[A]**

---

*   The letters in brackets at the end of each activity relate to the following: **A** = all ages; **Jr.** = grade-school age; **Sr.** = junior- and senior-high age; **G** = recommended for girls only; **B** = recommended for boys only.

➤ **Connect the Dots.** Give each camper pencil and paper, and have them make a grid of dots. Campers pair off in two's or three's for this game. Each player takes a turn connecting two dots (no diagonals).

When a player can close a box (complete the fourth side), he or she puts his or her initials in that box. The game ends when all the dots are connected to form boxes. The player who has the most initialed boxes is the winner. **[Jr.]**

➤ **Getting to Know You.** See the game under ALL-CAMP ACTIVITIES. This game has many variations. Create one that will fit your cabin group and have the camp office make the copies.

➤ **Know It All.** Each player is given a pencil and a full-size piece of paper. Across the top of the length-wise side of the paper, have them print a word such as **A C O R N**. The counselor now calls out "Animals" and each player writes down the names of as many animals as he or she can in each column with the first letter of the animal matching the column letter. For example, alligator and albatross is the A column.

Each player receives a point for each animal, PLUS a bonus point for each animal that no one else listed. Other categories could be flowers, birds, Bible characters, names, cities, and so forth. **[A]**

6

Active in-Cabin
Games for Small Spaces

The following is a list of activities* that involves the whole camp. These activities may be initiated by the Program Director or by the counselor working with the Director. Some are very simple but add memorable moments to the total camp experience.

➤ **Simon Says.** Everyone stands in a row in the cabin. The leader faces them or is at one end of the cabin. He or she tells them to do something like "put your hand on your head," or "touch your toes." If the leader precedes the command with "Simon Says," then everyone is to do it. "Simon Says" is left out of the command in order to trick the players. Any who obey when they should not, sit on a bunk until the next game. [Jr.]

➤ **Penny Candy Hunt.** Have all the campers hide under their blankets/sleeping bags. Quickly hide 30 or more pieces of penny candy in the cabin. After those in the top bunk stand on the floor, say "GO" for a fast and wild hunt. [Jr.]

* The letters in brackets at the end of each activity relate to the following: A = all ages; **Jr.** = grade-school age; **Sr.** = junior- and senior-high age; G = recommended for girls only; **B** = recommended for boys only.

➤   **Cooperative Spelling**. From your Treasure Chest, take out two sets of cards with letters. Each set is identical. Divide the cabin group into two equal teams (primarily by intelligence levels).

Each team member holds ONE letter facing forward. You have a list of words that these letters could spell on a 3" x 5" card. When you give the word, it is a contest to see which team can spell the word first. The players must shuffle around until the word is spelled out by facing you with their cards in front of them. [Jr.]

➤   **Balloon Stomp**. If you have adequate room in the cabin (be careful of sharp bed corners!), blow up a balloon for each camper and have them tie it to one of their ankles. At the "GO" signal, each one tries to stomp and break all the other balloons. [Jr.]

➤   **Balloon Volleyball**. If your cabin space allows this game, tie a string high across the middle. Divide the campers into two teams. Play volleyball with a balloon by using the string for a net. [A]

➤   **Indian Wrestling**. There are several variations of this. Use the ones that are SAFE in your group-living context:

☞ **Hand wrestling**. Stand on the floor with a line between the contestants. On signal, they reach out and shake hands, then each tries to pull the other over the line.

☞ **Arm wrestling**. Both contestants sit on opposite sides of the table or lay flat on the floor. With elbows down, clasp hands. Each tries to push the other one's hand to the surface of the table or ground.

☞ **Leg wrestling**. Both contestants lay flat on their backs, next to each other, in opposite directions, hip to hip. The inside leg is raised on the count of 1, 2, and 3. On 3, the legs are locked at the knee joint and each tries to pull the other over. Be sure to have some kind of cushion or mattress under the boys. [Jr. B]

➤ **Back-to-back Stunt**. Divide the cabin group into pairs. They sit on the floor back to back, lock arms at the elbows, and attempt to stand up together. After they practice this and can do it, combine two pairs to make it a foursome! If they can do it, add more! [Jr. B]

➤ **Soccer (Rainy-day Style)**. Arrange the beds in the cabin so that campers can sit on the beds and form two lines, facing each other. Each side is a team. With their legs extended, they should be able to just touch the other side's toes. At each end of these two parallel lines is a goal (a chair). Drop a ball (playground or nerf) in the middle. The object is for each team to try to kick the ball into their goal WHILE HANDS ARE CLASPED BEHIND THE BACK and all teammates remain seated. [Jr.]

➤   **Cooperation.** Rearrange your beds in the cabin so they form a channel, just 19 inches wide, down the middle of the cabin. It will probably only require two beds on each side for this game.

Line the players up between the beds. Number off. Emphasize that each player must keep his or her number. For younger players (or those who get confused easily) tape on their number.

The object is now to reverse the order of players so that number ten ends up where number one is now, and all players are in numerical order. NO ONE can step on the beds or use them as a help in any way! The player in the middle should end up right where he or she started.

After this is accomplished once, repeat it and try to beat the clock. There is a time penalty (add seconds to the score) for anyone who uses the beds. [A]

➤   **Hit the Can.** Arrange the setup for this game to fit your cabin or living space. It can be played between two lines of bunk beds.

Put a large trash can (three feet high, if you can get one) in the middle. One team (half of the cabin group) lies on their backs with their heads to the can. The other team stands behind a line about ten feet away (closer for younger campers). You can set this up so everyone is on one side of the can, or you can split it so there are two lines, each ten feet away from the can.

The players for the team on the floor each has a paper bat made of rolled up newspaper. The team behind the lines have a pile of newspapers to make into paper balls.

At the "GO" signal, one team makes paper balls and tries to throw them into the can, each one scoring a "basket." The other team is trying to bat them away. The team on the floor must keep their shoulders to the floor.

Set a two-minute limit, count the number of baskets made and then reverse the teams. This game is good for several rounds, but do not wear it out. [Jr. & Sr. B]

➤   **Pass It On.** Form a circle by sitting on the edge of a couple of beds. Give everyone some object from the cabin (a shoe, ball, book, broom, etc.). At the signal, everyone passes their object to the right. Keep everything moving at one time. If someone drops an object, they are out, BUT NOT THEIR OBJECT.

Soon there will be many more objects than people. The last one in the game is the winner. Counselor, be alert as to WHO dropped it, the passer or the receiver. [Jr.]

➤   **Scoop**. Use the same setup as the game, Pass It On, but number each player. Using a large lid or other disk object. Spin it in the middle of the group and call out one number. That person must pick up the lid before it stops spinning, and the person calling the number must try again. If the person called did not get the lid in time, then that person is now "It." [Jr.]

➤   **True or False**. Use the same setup as Pass It On, but have two teams facing each other. Each team is numbered off (i.e., 1 to 5). At each end of the isle is a chair. One is marked TRUE and the other is marked FALSE.

The counselor reads a question, and then calls a number. If the answer is TRUE, the two players with that number should race for the TRUE chair, and so forth. Each team gets a point for the correct answer IF the teammate gets to the chair first.

Before playing this game, have a list of questions ready. These questions can come from the

Bible or from the Bible lessons and chapel talks during this week at camp. [Jr.]

➤   **Room Scavenger Hunt.** Have ready two identical lists of things that can be found in the cabin. Divide the group into two and give each a list. At "GO," each team must bring the counselor each item on the list. The first team to find it all is the winner.

For the older campers, make the list more difficult such as a tooth (from a comb) or a picture of Lincoln (from a penny). [A]

7 NonActive Cabin Games

The following is a list of activities* that involves the whole camp. These activities may be initiated by the Program Director or by the counselor working with the Director. Some are very simple but add memorable moments to the total camp experience.

➤ **Let's Go Shopping.** The leader starts with, "The Camp Director went to town to buy a" and then names an item. The next person in line repeats the same thing and adds one more thing that needs to be bought. This can be played with everyone sitting around on the bunks. Just establish who follows whom. [Jr.]

➤ **20 Questions.** One person is "It." He or she has a famous person in mind from the Bible. Everyone tries to guess who it is by asking <u>Yes</u> and <u>No</u> questions. If the group cannot guess within 20 questions, "It" has another turn. [Jr.]

➤ **Name That Tune.** If you are good at singing or playing an instrument, hum or play the first

---

* The letters in brackets at the end of each activity relate to the following: A = all ages; **Jr.** = grade-school age; **Sr.** = junior- and senior-high age; **G** = recommended for girls only; **B** = recommended for boys only.

measure of familiar songs. It is a contest to see who can guess the song first. If they don't get it, do it again and add a measure.

Use many songs that have been sung at camp and other familiar hymns. Do NOT use secular songs. [A]

➤   **Ready Rhythm.** Sit in a circle (on the edge of the lower bunk beds, perhaps). The leader starts the rhythm by slapping his or her hands on their thigh, then clapping once, then snapping right fingers, then snapping left fingers. Repeat thigh, clap, right, left.

After everyone is with the leader in repeating this rhythm, the leader says his/her own name when snapping the right fingers, and then says another person's name when snapping the left fingers. The person named must do the same thing — say his/her own name on the right snap and another person's name on the left.

If a player whose name was called does NOT keep the rhythm first with their own name, then the name of another, that player rotates to the end. All the players move up a seat. The object is to get to the #1 seat. This game is NOT recommended for children under nine because of the fast decision making required. [A]

➤   **Pantomime.** Pantomime verbs, Bible characters, stories. Be sensitive to the desires of your group. Some kids love it, and some hate it. If you love it, this activity may do well. **[A]**

➤   **This Is My Nose.** The leader or person chosen as "It" stands in front of the group and points to some part of his or her body, but calls it by some other part. The player who is addressed by the leader must point to the part of their body named by the leader, but the player must call it the part to which the leader pointed. Example: Leader points to his or her foot, "This is my head. 1, 2, 3, 4, 5, 6, 7, 8, 9, 10." Camper must also point to their head and say "This is my foot" before the leader counts to 10. **[Jr.]**

➤   **Zip Zap** . Campers sit in a circle. One player, however, stands in the middle. That player points to someone and says, "Zip 1, 2, 3, 4, 5, 6, 7, 8, 9, 10!" Before the player reaches ten, the one sitting and pointed to must give the name of the person on their right. If the player in the middle says "Zap...," then the name of the person on the left must be given. If the one sitting does not do it correctly, then that person becomes "It." **[Jr.]**

➤   **Knots.** In your Treasure Chest, have a set of ropes for each camper. Use these to practice knot tying. Most boys will enjoy the challenge. A chart of knots and how they are made would be helpful. [Jr. B]

➤   **The Living Mirror.** Two campers at a time face each other. One does the action and the other must be the mirror and do exactly the same, but reversed, as in a mirror. Special recognition goes to the team that can do it the best. [A]

➤   **Who Am I?** Put a sign on each person's back with the name of a person from the Bible. Each person asks <u>Yes</u> and <u>No</u> questions of everyone else to try to guess what name is on their back. This game can be repeated with other names, Bible places, Bible events, names of food and so forth. The entire set of names should be the same theme. [A]

➤   **Who's the Leader.** One person is sent out of the room. Everyone is seated in a circle. Another person is chosen (by the counselor) as the leader. The leader is going to lead the group in a series of actions (clapping, stomping, winking, waving, etc.). When the "It" person comes back into the group, he or she must guess who the leader is as the leader leads the group in these different actions. [Jr.]

➤   **Fast Counter.** Pair the campers off in two's. The counselor can fill in it to make it even. Each pair stands facing each other with hands behind their backs. At the signal, both quickly put their hands in front of their faces with a number of fingers up. A closed fist is zero.

The first of the pair to give the correct total number of fingers on all four hands wins the round. The best in two out of three rounds is the winner of the game. Then have the winners and losers pair up. Keep going until a champion FAST COUNTER results. [Jr.]

➤ **You're Hot**. One person is "It" and must hide in the corner or under his or her covers while someone else hides an object in the cabin. When ready, "It" starts looking for the object. When "It" moves closer to the object, the whole group hums a song louder, and if "It" moves away from the object, they hum softer and softer. Choose a song that is sung often in camp this week. The object of the game is to see who can find the object the fastest. So time each player. [Jr.]

➤ **Do You Have the Power?** There are a number of games that deal with knowing the inside secret. For these games, at least two people must know the secret. One leaves the room, something is chosen, the one who left comes back in and must guess what was chosen after a few questions are asked.

☞ **Black magic**. The one asking questions points to a black object just before the chosen object is asked.

☞   **Red, white, and blue.** Play it just like Black Magic. Except for the first time, the chosen object follows something that is red, the next time it follows something that is white, and the third time it follows something that is blue. Then rotate once again red, white, and blue.

☞   **Book magic.** The one asking questions points to a book just before the chosen object.

☞   **Knife, fork and spoon.** One person leaves the room. Someone in the room is chosen to be the mystery person. "It" comes back into the room. The leader arranges a knife, fork, and spoon on the floor in a certain way. "It" guesses the correct person. How? The leader sits in exactly the same position as the mystery person. The knife, fork, and spoon have NOTHING to do with it! "It" matches the leaders position with the mystery person.

☞   **Smell the broom.** After "It" leaves the room, a spot is chosen on a broom handle. When "It" comes back into the room, he or she smells the broom until they finds the right spot. How? "It" is really watching the feet of the leader. When the feet move even a little, that is the spot. Hint: mark the broom handle using magic marker with different letters or numbers. [A]

➤   **Air, Land, Water, Fire**. Players sit in a circle (as on lower bunks). The leader stands in the middle and then suddenly points to a player and says one of the four: air, land, water, or fire. The player must then name an animal that lives in that environment BEFORE the leader counts to 10. If "fire" is called, the player says nothing. If the player loses, he is "It." For variation use bird, beast or fish. **[A]**

8   How to Clean up Quickly

Before an activity, everyone is anxious to help. AFTER the activity, the mood has changed. No one wants to clean up and put the place back in order again. You need to be ready.

Part of preparation is planning for the cleanup.

If you can do it all yourself, quickly and efficiently, do it. Have the sacks, bags or boxes ready to store the supplies, equipment or trash.

A more elaborate activity often needs a number of hands to get the job done. Here are two easy ways to get the help you need:

1.   Before starting the activity, give 3" x 5" card notes to those people you want helping you. Be specific as to what you want them to do. For example: "After this next game, please help put the paper in trash cans," or "After the Rhythm game, please help put the chairs back in order and collect any pencils and paper lying around," or "After the County Fair, please help Dan put the recreation equipment away."

2.   If it was a simple game time, end the last game; but before anyone can move, give specific responsibilities to several participants to help clean up and put things back in order. This method works well with any group of under 40 participants.

Whatever method you choose, do plan ahead to clean up any mess and to put away all the equipment and props. If you are involved in an ongoing program with a busy schedule, this pre-planning is very important in order to stay one step ahead of the campers.

9 How to Evaluate Your Performance

It is all over. You did it. All the planning, gathering materials, preparing the area, and actually running the activity is past history. How did you do? How well did your activity go over with the campers? Do you feel elated and satisfied, or defeated and depressed?

To increase your ability in recreational leadership, take the time (and the humility pills) needed to evaluate what happened. Here are a few questions to ask yourself:

Okay	Needs Help	
___	___	Did most of the participants have an enjoyable time? (There will always be one or two who make it their business to have a boring time.)
___	___	Did the activity MOVE along and not drag? If it was a party or game time, did I move quickly and efficiently from one activity to the next without dead time in between?
___	___	Were all the props and equipment at hand when I needed them?
___	___	Did I have all the game instructions either memorized or on cards?

____ ____   Did I have all the game instructions either memorized or on cards?

____ ____   Did I get the help I needed? Did I tell others ahead of time what I was expecting out of them?

____ ____   Did I have the area set up for the activity?

____ ____   Did I maintain a positive mental attitude, even if some participants were negative?

____ ____   Did the activities fit the age-group?

____ ____   Did the activities fit the space available?

____ ____   Did the activities fit the mood of the group?

____ ____   Did the activities fit the needs of the group (i.e., active, quiet, mental)?

____ ____   Did the activities fit the time available?

____ ____   If it was a game time, did I stop the game when I saw the first signs of a few campers starting to lose interest?

____ ____   Did I plan plenty of activities for the time allowed? Did I have some extra activities?

____ ____   Was I flexible in adapting, changing, or even dropping activities so that I met the needs or changing situation?

____ ____   Did I maintain self-control and group-control?

Was your game time a flop? Don't worry!

As you look back over what happened, it may be that your conclusion is this: "What a flop!" That can be very discouraging. It has happened to me on several occasions. Sometimes I was only half satisfied, because the experience could have been a whole lot better.

One key to success is using your own evaluations. "O.K., so it flopped. Why? What could I have done to make it only a half-flop"?

Then take the opportunity to try again, but do not repeat the same mistakes. Learn by your evaluations.

Sometimes a partial or total flop was not even your fault. These things can happen and destroy all your plans:

- Was there a strong and leading element (core group) in your group that was fighting against you with negativism, complaining or even non-cooperation?

- Was the space so small and crowded that little could be done?

- Were the kids too tired (or too hyped up) to do anything?

- Was there a continuing outside disturbance that prohibited group attention?

- Were the other adults that were supposed to help you only distracting the group and not giving you real cooperation?

These things are out of your control. In such situations you need to think fast and adapt your program to fit the uncomfortable situation. The bottom line is simply to do the best you can and make the best of it. Don't be too hard on yourself.

If you will evaluate after each experience, write down what you learned, and apply it at the next opportunity, I think you will find your ability as a recreational leader steadily increasing. Use each "disaster" as a stepping stone to success. Use each success as a pattern for further growth.

I find great satisfaction in helping others to have a good time. Follow the suggestions in this book and you will too!

Order Form

If you would like more copies of this book, please tear out this order form and enclose it with a check made out to the BENJAMIN PUBLISHING CO. Alternatively, you may telephone 508-425-4055 to order direct. All orders are backed by an unconditional one-year return privilege. Please inquire, if interested, about the quantity discount schedule.

Quantity	Item	Unit Price	Total
	How to Be a Successful Camp Counselor	$9.95	
	The Camp Counselor's Handbook of Over 90 Games and Activities Just for Rainy Days!	5.95	

Tax of 5% applies to Massachusetts residents only.
U.S. shipping (UPS): $3.00 first item, $.50 each additional. UPS 2nd day is $7.00 first item, $1.00 each additional.
Canadian shipping (air mail): $5.00 first item, $1.00 each aditional.
Overseas shipping (air mail): $10.00 each item.

Subtotal	
Tax	
Shipping	
Total	

Name		
Camp/Church/Company		
Address		
City	State	Zip
Phone ( ) —		

BENJAMIN PUBLISHING COMPANY
P.O. Box 488
Fredonian Street
Shirley, MA 01464

Order Form

If you would like more copies of this book, please tear out this order form and enclose it with a check made out to the BENJAMIN PUBLISHING CO. Alternatively, you may telephone 508-425-4055 to order direct. All orders are backed by an unconditional one-year return privilege. Please inquire, if interested, about the quantity discount schedule.

Quantity	Item	Unit Price	Total
	How to Be a Successful Camp Counselor	$9.95	
	The Camp Counselor's Handbook of Over 90 Games and Activities Just for Rainy Days!	5.95	

Tax of 5% applies to Massachusetts residents only.
U.S. shipping (UPS): $3.00 first item, $.50 each additional. UPS 2nd day is $7.00 first item, $1.00 each additional.
Canadian shipping (air mail): $5.00 first item, $1.00 each aditional.
Overseas shipping (air mail): $10.00 each item.

Subtotal	
Tax	
Shipping	
Total	

Name		
Camp/Church/Company		
Address		
City	State	Zip
Phone ( ) —		

BENJAMIN PUBLISHING COMPANY
P.O. Box 488
Fredonian Street
Shirley, MA 01464